**Please Note: This is an unofficial conversation starters guide.
If you have not yet read the original work, please do so first.**

**Copyright © 2015 by dailyBooks. All Rights Reserved.
First Published in the United States of America 2015**

We hope you enjoy this complementary guide from **dailyBooks.** *We
aim to provide quality, thought provoking material to assist in
your discovery and discussions on some of today's favorite books.*

Disclaimer / Terms of Use: Product names, logos, brands, and other trademarks
featured or referred to within this publication are the property of their respective
trademark holders and are not affiliated with dailyBooks. The publisher and
author make no representations or warranties with respect to the accuracy or
completeness of these contents and disclaim all warranties such as warranties of
fitness for a particular purpose. This guide is unofficial and unauthorized. It is
not authorized, approved, licensed, or endorsed by the original book's author or
publisher and any of their licensees or affiliates.

No part of this publication may be reproduced or retransmitted, electronic or
mechanical, without the written permission of the publisher.

D1466580

Tips for Using dailyBooks Conversation Starters:

EVERY GOOD BOOK CONTAINS A WORLD FAR DEEPER THAN the surface of its pages. The characters and their world come alive through the words on the pages, yet the characters and its world still live on. Questions herein are designed to bring us beneath the surface of the page and invite us into the world that lives on. These questions can be used to:

- Foster a deeper understanding of the book
- Promote an atmosphere of discussion for groups
- Assist in the study of the book, either individually or corporately
- Explore unseen realms of the book as never seen before

About Us:

THROUGH YEARS OF EXPERIENCE AND FIELD EXPERTISE, from newspaper featured book clubs to local library chapters, *dailyBooks* can bring your book discussion to life. Host your book party as we discuss some of today's most widely read books.

Conversations

on

Between the World and Me

Ta-Nehisi Coates

By dailyBooks

FREE Download: Bonus Books Included
*Claim Yours with **Any Purchase** of* Conversation Starters!

How to claim your free download:

1. **LEAVE MY AMAZON REVIEW.**
You Can Also Use the "Write a Customer Review" Button

2. **ENTER YOUR BEST EMAIL HERE.**
NO SPAM. Your Email is Never Shared and is Protected

Or Scan QR Code

3. **RECEIVE YOUR FREE DOWNLOAD.**
Download is Delivered Instantly to Inbox

Table of Contents

Introducing *Between the World and Me*

IN 2015, *BETWEEN THE WORLD AND ME* BY TA-NEHISI COATES was published by Spiegel & Grau. This book presented itself as a series of letters dedicated to the author's teenage son. The whole concept of the novel is to expose the reality of what it really takes to be black in a society full of white people. Coates depicted in the novel that there is a present physical danger for those whose color is different from the rest. He recollects a certain autobiographical account of his teenage life in Baltimore, which takes inspiration from the novel *The Fire Next Time* by James Baldwin way back in the year 1993. It is clear in the book that Ta-Nehisi Coates believes that there hasn't and never will be any racial justness in the American Society for black people.

Between the World and Me is a vicious portrayal of the African-American predicament. Ta-Nehisi wrote with severe abjection towards racism in his society as his novel is not the common racism story, but rather an attack on the system which has long made the lives of his likes to be worthless. Ta-Nehisi Coates' book has shown to be a popular work, proven by the many awards that it has received from prestigious award-giving bodies, such as the National Book Award and the like. Its blunt subjects and themes have induced mixed emotions for its readers. The book's critique has also made this book a success. It stands out from the common flow of other books about racism on the market. *Between the World and Me* is "raw" and interesting.

Slavery within the African-American race has never been a secret; however, there is a big difference between simply knowing this and reading the words of those who have experienced it first hand—their anxiety and anger painting a picture for the readers.

Introducing the Author

THE AUTHOR OF *BETWEEN THE WORLD AND ME* IS AN American writer and journalist, as well as an educator named Ta-Nehisi Paul Coates. Being a national correspondent for *The Atlantic*, he writes about varied types of social and cultural issues, particularly African-Americans. Being an experienced journalist, Coates has been part of numerous well-known publications, such as the *New York Times*, the *Washington Post*, the *Village Voice*, and the *Washington Monthly*, among other publications. He received the "Genius Grant" from the John D. and Catherine T. MacArthur Foundation in 2015.

Between the World and Me is Ta-Nehisi Coates' second book. It functions as a sequel to his published memoir, *The Beautiful Struggle: A Father, Two Sons, and an Unlikely Road to Manhood,* which was released in 2008. His second book won the 2015 National Book Award for Non-fiction.

Coates was born in Baltimore, Maryland. His father is a Vietnam War veteran named William "Paul" Coates, and his mother is a teacher named Cheryl Waters. Ta-Nehisi's father founded the *Black Classic Press*, which is a publication that specializes in African- American titles.

Ta-Nehisi Coates' father has seven children in all, by four different women. Unlike his other siblings, who most often lived with their mothers, Ta-Nehisi was with his father most of the time. However, it is also to be noted that Coates said that the children were raised in a close-knit family.

Coates' interest in books was instilled in him at an early age because his mother, a teacher at that time, obliged him to write essays as his consequence for unpleasant behavior. His father's works in the *Black Classic Press* also influenced him a lot as a novelist, taking into account that he has read most of the books

that have been published by his father.

Discussion Questions

. . . .

question 1

The main theme of *Between the World and Me* is manhood. Do
you think it would have been more appropriate for the author if
he had incorporated the struggle of the African-American
females in the book? Why or why not?

. . . .

question 2

Coates said in the book, "The schools were not concerned with curiosity" but rather with "compliance." What does this statement depict of the American educational institution at the time? Can these lines from the novel be predicted as a plea for reform of the education system?

. . . .

question 3

Coates' deviated from the usual anatomy of characterizing people as either good or bad; instead, he used the terms "pure and dark intentions." In connection with this, how would you explain Coates' point of view in terms of humanity's complexity? Give examples.

question 4

Between the World and Me mentioned the term "people" as a word that politically refers to those who "believe themselves white." What type of disunity of race does the United States have as it becomes progressive?

question 5

In connection with the previous question, how would reminding people that race is solely a social construction help in this kind of situation?

. . . .

question 6

What are the diverse sides of the "The Dream" as the author of
the book calls them? What are problems that can be seen in each
angle?

. . . .

question 7

Coates wrote in the book, "The struggle is really all that I have for you"… "because it is the only portion of this world under your control." In your opinion, would you consider these statements to be pessimistic or hopeful? Explain.

. . . .

question 8

The book talks about the problematic society in which the author belongs, do you think it might have been more helpful for the reader if the author had discussed solutions to the problem? Why or why not?

. . . .

. . . .

question 9

The book is grounded on social injustice raised by color. Do you think this type of injustice and discrimination still exists today? Cite examples.

. . . .

. . . .

question 10

Between the World and Me is a series of letters written for the author's teenage son. How do you think this type of "arrangement" helped readers of the book appreciate its concept more?

. . . .

question 11

Coates wrote on page 7 of his book, "But race is the child of racism, not the father." In this, he seems to imply that race will not exist without racism. Do you agree? Why or why not?

. . . .

question 12

Coates wrote on page 71 of his novel, "Perhaps struggle is all we
have because the god of history is an atheist, and nothing about
his world is meant to be." What do you think the author means?

. . . .

question 13

On page 120 of the book, Coates wrote, "In America, the injury is not being born with darker skin, with fuller lips, with a broader nose, but in everything that happens after." What do you think he meant by this?

question 14

What is the moral lesson of the book *Between the World and Me*?

. . . .

question 15

In what ways can we bring these moral lessons into our own
battle against racial discrimination?

. . . .

. . . .

question 16

Between the World and Me won the National Book Award for the year 2005. What do you think made this book stand out from the rest of the best-selected literary features that year?

. . . .

. . . .

question 17

Coates wrote *Between the World and Me* following a meeting with President Barack Obama. What do you think inspired the author to write this book after the meeting?

. . . .

question 18

Between the World and Me got its title in a poem written by Richard Wright. What do you think is the reason Coates chose this title for the book? How is the title connected with the message conveyed it?

. . . .

question 19

According to John Legend in the *Wall Street Journal*, the book is "a look at the racial history" and "powerful and emotional." Do you agree with his review? Why or why not?

. . . .

. . . .

question 20

The book ended with the story of Mabel Jones, daughter of a sharecropper. Do you think this story gave a justified ending for the book? Why or Why not?

. . . .

FREE Download: Bonus Books Included
*Claim Yours with **Any Purchase** of* Conversation Starters!

How to claim your free download:

4.   LEAVE MY AMAZON REVIEW.
You Can Also Use "Write a Customer Review" Button

Leave My Review

5.   ENTER YOUR BEST EMAIL HERE.
NO SPAM. Your Email is Never Shared and is Protected

Or Scan Above

6.   RECEIVE YOUR FREE DOWNLOAD.
Download is Instantly Delivered to Inbox

. . . .

question 21

Toni Morrison, a novelist, wrote that Ta-Nehisi Coates fills the "intellectual void" left by James Baldwin 28 years ago. What do you think Morrison meant by saying such?

. . . .

question 22

Benjamin Wallace-Wells of New York stated that a certain fear for one's child hovers the book and that Coates' atheism gave the book some sense of urgency to its readers. Do you agree with his review? Why or Why not?

. . . .

question 23

According to Michiko Kakutani of the *New York Times*, the book seems to be a sequel to Coate's 2008 memoir. Do you think there will be other books to follow this sequel? Why or why not?

. . . .

question 24

Michiko Kakutani felt that Coates did not acknowledge consistently the racial progress that can be seen nowadays. Do you agree? Why or why not?

question 25

Washington University in St. Lois and the University of Kansas selected *Between the World and Me* as a must-read book for their students for the fall 2016 semester. Do you think this is a good book for college students? Why or Why not?

. . . .

question 26

Coates left Howard University after five years to start a
journalism career, making him the only member of his family
who doesn't have a college degree. Do you think this was a good
decision for him? What are the advantages and disadvantages of
Ta-Nehisi Coates' decision?

. . . .

question 27

Coates' first name, Ta-Nehisi, means Nubia an Egyptian term for "land of the black." Do you think this name suits the writer? In what ways does his name truly signify his works and passion?

question 28

Coates earnestly believes less in the sense of eventual justice but rather he shouts for urgency in his books. Why do you think this way of writing is effective? In what cases would it be not effective?

. . . .

question 29

Coates received a "Genius Grant" from John D. and Catherine T. MacArthur Foundation in 2015. In what ways does Coates' "Geniusness" come through in *Between the World and Me*?

. . . .

question 30

Some consider *Between the World and Me* a "brave" literary piece because it fearlessly recapitulates that violence scourged in the black skin dated back in history up to our time. Do you think the style of the author is best this way, or would it be better if he had "shed a little light" to whatever improvements the American society has to offer regarding racial discrimination?

. . . .

· ·

question 31

If you were the author of *Between the World and Me*, would you use the same strategy of making it a series of letters to your son? Why or why not?

· ·

question 32

The title of *Between the World and Me* came from James Baldwin's *The Fire Next Time*. If you were the author of the book, would you have chosen the same title or would you have chosen another one? What would it be and why?

· ·

. . . .

question 33

The story ends with a story about a Mabel Jones. If you were the author of this book, how would you choose to end the book?

. . . .

. . . .

question 34

The book contains a realistic point of view and doesn't aim for a
latter sense of social justice, but rather to the citizens to be acting
"now." If you were the author of the book, would you do it in the
same way? Or would you take into account any improvement
that the social pedal has had as of the moment? Explain.

. . . .

. . . .

question 35

The author believes that the stories of injustice in the American society are usually rooted on African-American people. How do you think society would be different today if "whites" had a history of being slaves?

. . . .

. . . .

question 36

If you were the author, would you write the book focusing on the fear that other people have brought you, or would you write it differently focusing on the good things that your race has done, and why?

. . . .

. . . .

question 37

In the book, the writer wrote letters to his son. Who would you write to and why?

. . . .

question 38

If you were the author of the book, how would you have started and ended the story? Would you change a lot about how it was written?

Quiz Questions

. . . .

question 39

True or False: The overlying theme of the book *Between the World and Me* is the injustice suffered by the African-American people in the American Society.

. . . .

question 40

True or False: Coates said in the book that schools are more concerned with curiosity rather than with compliance.

. . . .

question 41

True or False: Coates used the usual way of categorizing people to be either good or bad in his book *Between the World and Me.*

. . . .

question 42

The book is a series of letters for the author's _____ so he can appreciate the societal freedom that he has right now.

question 43

True or False: Coates said in the book, "But race is the child of racism, not the father."

question 44

True or False: Coates said in his book, "In America, the injury is not being born with darker skin, with fuller lips, with a broader nose but in everything that happens after."

question 45

Coates wrote, "Perhaps struggle is all we have because the god of history is _____, and nothing about this world is meant to be"

question 46

True or False: Ta-Nehisi Coates received his college degree from Howard University; he is said to be the first in his family to have a college degree.

question 47

True or False: Coates received the "Genius Grant" from John D. and Catherine T. Foundation in the year 2015.

question 48

Coates name Ta-Nehisi means "land of the _____."

. . . .

question 49

True or False: Coates earnestly believes in the sense of eventual justice.

. . . .

question 50

True or False: Coates thinks that Richard Baldwin's literary entitled *The Fire Next Day* is one of the author's main inspirations for the book.

Quiz Answers

1. True
2. False; Coates said, "The schools were not concerned with curiosity" but rather with "compliance."
3. False; he used the terms "pure and dark intentions."
4. Son
5. True
6. True
7. an atheist
8. False; Coates did not finish his degree.
9. True
10. Black
11. False
12. True

THE END

Want to promote your book group? Register here.

PLEASE LEAVE US A FEEDBACK.

THANK YOU!

FREE Download: Bonus Books Included
*Claim Yours with **<u>Any Purchase</u>** of Conversation Starters!*

How to claim your free download:

7. <u>LEAVE MY AMAZON REVIEW.</u>
You Can Also Use "Write a Customer Review" Button

Leave My Review

8. <u>ENTER YOUR BEST EMAIL HERE.</u>
NO SPAM. Your Email is Never Shared and is Protected

Or Scan Above

9.   RECEIVE YOUR FREE DOWNLOAD.
Download is Instantly Delivered to Inbox

Made in the USA
Monee, IL
18 May 2021

68866588R10039